Half-Time Highlights
A Guide to Dancing in the NBA/NFL

By Ashley Worrell

www.half-timehighlights.com

Note to the Reader: My reasoning for writing this book was to share my personal experiences and perhaps help others wanting to follow the same path. When I began auditioning, there were not a lot of resources to research dancing for the NFL or NBA. Everything I learned, I learned by training, traveling, and physical research. My hope is to help aide you in your quest for dancing, and perhaps, living your dreams.

Half-Time Highlights
How to Prepare to Dance in the NBA/NFL

Chapter I

The Beginning

"In actual life every great enterprise begins with and takes its first forward steps in faith."

-Fredrick von Schlegel

The History of Cheerleading

Different reports credit the Colts, Packers, or Steelers with
the first cheerleading squads- dating back as far as 1931- but, let's be
honest- NFL Cheerleaders as we now see them were invented by the
Cowboys.

The story goes that the Cowboys originally hired models, but
quickly realized that the women had to be attractive, yes, but also
entertain. So in the early 1970s they started hiring women based on
looks and dancing ability... They went national during Super Bowl X
when the TV broadcast kept showing the Cowboys' Cheerleaders,
and almost immediately teams around the league began forming
cheerleading squads to mirror the Cowboys'. [1]

---

[1] The Kansas City Star August 30, 2009

History

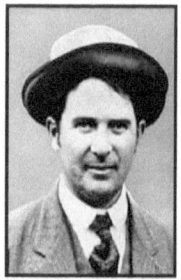

Minnesota Gopher Cheerleader Johnny Campbell

"Princeton graduate Thomas Peebles introduced the idea of organized crowds cheering at football games to the University of Minnesota. However, it was not until 1898 that University of Minnesota student Johnny Campbell directed a crowd in cheering "Rah, Rah, Rah! Sku-u-mar, Hoo-Rah! Hoo-Rah! Varsity! Varsity! Varsity, Minn-e-So-Tah!", making Campbell the very first cheerleader and November 2, 1898 the official birth date of organized cheerleading. Soon after, the University of Minnesota organized a "yell leader" squad of 6 male students, who still use Campbell's original cheer today. In 1903 the first cheerleading fraternity, Gamma Sigma was founded. Cheerleading started out as an all-male activity, but females began participating in 1923, due to limited availability of female collegiate sports. At this time, gymnastics, tumbling, and megaphones were incorporated into popular cheers, and are still used today. Today it is estimated that 97% of cheerleading participants overall are female, but males still make up 50% of cheering squads at the collegiate level.

In 1948, Lawrence "Herkie" Herkimer, of Dallas, TX and a former cheerleader at Southern Methodist University formed the *National Cheerleaders Association (NCA)* as a way to hold cheerleading clinics. In 1949, The NCA held its first clinic in Huntsville, TX with 52 girls in attendance. "Herkie" contributed many firsts to the sport: the founding of the *Cheerleader & Danz Team* cheerleading uniform supply company, inventing the herkie, (where one leg is bent towards the ground and the other is out to the side as high as it will stretch in the toe-touch position) and creating the "Spirit Stick". By the 1960s, college cheerleaders began hosting workshops across the nation, teaching fundamental cheer skills to eager high-school-age girls. In 1965, Fred Gastoff invented the vinyl pom-pon and it was introduced into competitions by the International Cheerleading Foundation (now the World Cheerleading Association or WCA). Organized cheerleading competitions began to pop up with the first ranking of the "Top Ten College Cheerleading Squads" and "Cheerleader All America" awards given out by the International Cheerleading Foundation in 1967. In 1978, America was introduced to competitive cheerleading by the first broadcast of Collegiate Cheerleading Championships on CBS.

In the 1960s National Football League (NFL) teams began to organize professional cheerleading teams. The Baltimore Colts (now the Indianapolis Colts) was the first NFL team to have an organized cheerleading squad. It was the Dallas Cowboys Cheerleaders who gained the spotlight with their revealing outfits and sophisticated dance moves, which debuted in the 1972-1973 season, but were first seen widely in Super Bowl X (1976). This caused the image of cheerleaders to permanently change, with many other NFL teams emulating them. Most of the professional teams' cheerleading squads would more accurately be described as dance teams by today's standards; as they rarely, if ever, actively encourage crowd noise or perform modern cheerleading moves.

The 1980s saw the onset of modern cheerleading with more difficult stunt sequences and gymnastics being incorporated into routines. All-star teams started to pop up, and with them the creation of the United States All-Star Federation (USASF) ESPN first broadcasted the National High School Cheerleading Competition nationwide in 1983. Cheerleading organizations such as the American Association of Cheerleading Coaches and Advisors (AACCA), founded in 1987, started applying universal safety standards to decrease the number of injuries and prevent dangerous stunts, pyramids and tumbling passes from being included in routines. In 2003, the National Council for Spirit Safety and Education (NCSSE) was formed to offer safety training for youth, school, all star and college coaches. The NCAA requires college cheer coaches to successfully complete a nationally recognized safety-training program. The NCSSE or AACCA certification programs are both recognized by the NCAA.

Even with its' athletic and competitive development, cheerleading at the school level has retained its' ties to the spirit leading traditions started back in the 1890s. Cheerleaders are seen as ambassadors for their schools, and leaders among the student body. At the college level, cheerleaders are often invited to help at university fundraisers.

Today, cheerleading is most closely associated with American football and basketball. Sports such as association football (soccer), ice hockey, volleyball, baseball, and wrestling sometimes sponsor cheerleading squads. The ICC Twenty20 Cricket World Cup in South Africa in 2007 was the first international cricket event to have cheerleaders. The Florida Marlins were the first Major League Baseball team to have cheerleaders. Debuting in 2003, the "Marlin Mermaids" gained national exposure and have influenced other MLB teams to develop their own cheer/dance squads.[2]

---

[2] Official History given by Wikipedia

My Story

My story is not unlike many other little girls. I began dancing in the studio when I was 3 years old, and I believe that I probably danced as soon as I could walk. I can honestly tell you that I have never imagined myself doing anything different. I never knew *exactly* how I would use dance, but I knew that I eventually wanted to own my own dance studio.

From what my mother tells me, I was not exactly Fred Astaire when it came to dancing. In fact, I had such an attention deficit, that she would have to attend the classes with me to learn the routines and teach me at home. In middle school, I was always a half count behind. But one thing never changed. That was my *love* for dance.

In middle school, I attended a studio that was fairly known in the Kansas City area. They had a competition team called the "Starz" and I remember so desperately wanting to be a part of the team. However, you had to be invited to be on the squad, and I was easily overlooked. I was very awkward, not a great dancer, and my looks were not too appealing at that time (well I was STILL in middle school!). This was my first memory of politics in the dance world. I remember feeling so hurt and left out, which eventually led me to a smaller studio. I think the worst part about the whole ordeal was to have not been given a *chance*.

I continued dancing in high school, and was soon exposed to the "pom squad". I had absolutely no desire to try out for this team until my junior year. For the first two years of high school, I had always thought the girls on the squad had a bad (or should I say, trampy) reputation. But, the more that I learned about the squad, that misconception could not have been farther from the truth. At the end of my sophomore year, I decided I would try out and see what this squad was all about. Before the actual auditions, the school held an audition open to the public the Wednesday before. Talk about intimidating! Every girl had to perform a two minute solo in front of the student body and it was my first exposure to dancing all by myself. I will never forget that experience because I learned so many things from it. I learned that when I was pressured into performing, I actually danced harder and my moves were cleaner. My adrenaline rush actually made my performance *better*!

Needless to say, I made the squad that year. In fact, I also made it my senior year, and cannot imagine my life without being on that squad. Besides the wonderful friendships that I made, I learned that performing was a huge rush and I lived for game days and nights.

Definitions

*Pom Squads usually consist of 8 to 18 dancers. You'll see them performing on the sidelines during football games and at time-outs, quarter-breaks, and sometimes half-times of basketball games. Pom, funk/hip hop, jazz, and novelty routines are the favorites of pom squads. Strong, tight arm motions and "athletic dancing" are what make a pom squad unique. This style of dance is close to cheerleader dancing.

*Dance Teams and Dance/Drill Teams are usually larger teams and have anywhere from 30 to 100 members. Like dance teams, you'll see them at half-time of football and basketball games. Because these teams are larger, they use formations and pattern work to accentuate their precision jazz, military, kick and prop during football season, dance/drill teams will highlight specialties within the team at competitions by performing lyrical, pom, modern and sometimes funk/hip hop routines as well. The Kilgore College Rangerettes were introduced in 1940 and continue to maintain the tradition today!

*Dance Teams can range from 16 to 30 members. A big trend we see in dance teams is that many teams' members also take lessons together at a dance studio. Because of this studio influence, dance teams tend to perform progressive, technically challenging choreography with an emphasis on jazz.[3]

NBA Dancers and NFL Cheerleaders. Today, both are considered "dance teams". In the beginning, NFL teams had cheerleaders, and many were co-ed. Since the field is so large for football, NFL cheerleaders would be under the category of pom squads- thus incorporating cheerleading moves with dance moves. They also incorporate more vocal cheering than NBA dancers. NBA dancers would lean more toward the last dance team definition, using a strong emphasis in jazz and hip hop.

---

[3] *Definitions by Dance Spirit Fall 1997

Chapter 2

Making the Move

"Change is not made without inconvenience, even from worse to better."

Richard Hooker

My dad always told me you can't make money by staying at home. With that said, I believe you have to go to know. Many cities do not have opportunities to dance, so you must be willing to travel and/or relocate.

Requirements

The following list is requirements needed to audition for most NBA/NFL Dance Teams:

- Must be at least 18 years old by tryout date (some require applicants to be 21 years old)
- Must have a high school degree or GED
- Able to attend all practices, games, and appearances
- Must have reliable transportation
- Live close, or willing to move, to location of the team

Keep your sense of humor. There's enough stress in the rest of your life to let bad shots ruin a game you're supposed to enjoy. Amy Strum Alcott

Chapter 3

First Audition

"We grow great by dreams. All big men are dreamers. They see things in the soft haze of a spring day or in the red fire of a long winter's evening.

Some of us let these great dreams die, but others nourish and protect them; nurse them through bad days till they bring them to the sunshine and light which comes always to those who hope that their dreams will come true."

Woodrow Wilson

In 1999, I had my first professional audition for the NBA Dallas Mavericks Dance Team. I had NO clue what I was getting myself into! There were a few friends of mine also trying out, so the process was a little easier to bare. I showed up to the audition about an hour early and there was already a line of at least 75 girls. My memory of the ladies trying out was completely intimidating. Most of the women were beautiful and thin. I felt very challenged to not be instantly insecure.

We were each given a number after we had submitted head and body shot photos, along with an application and our resume. After passing the registration tables, we were herded through the doors to a sea of women and camera crews. No amount of training could keep me from wanting to run out through those doors! Somehow, the thrill of a good challenge started my adrenaline going. My thought process was simply this: if I don't make this squad, I at least want to make the other girls earn it! (Did I mention I was competitive?!?)

I really had no clue of what to expect. I knew the basics: what I needed to bring, wear, and that I would be dancing. That was pretty much all that I knew. One other small detail: 14 to 16 girls would be selected out of 300+ women auditioning. Just a *small* detail!

I did not make the squad, but what I did was take away very valuable information for the next tryout. I vowed to myself that I would never be unprepared again. The following year, I took prep classes- 8 hours a week. I never missed a class or an opportunity to show my face. I hired a trainer to get my body in the best shape possible and to educate me on a nutrition plan. By the next audition, the director knew my face and my dance capabilities. I was 100% more prepared and I had earned a spot on the team.

Chapter 4

Preparing for Auditions

"To accomplish great things,

we must not only act but also dream,

not only plan but also believe."

Exercise

Training is probably the single most important thing you can do for a dance audition. The best advice I can give is to take as many jazz, hip hop, and prep classes you can find. If you cannot take with adults only, take that humbling step and take with kids! Strong technique can be seen within 5 minutes of an audition. Posture can help tremendously and can give an err of confidence.

Exercising at least 5 times a week can help build your endurance for long auditions. Judges will notice if you are physically spent after doing the routine only one time. They are looking for girls that can physically take dancing for 3+ hours. Building cardio endurance as well as strength training play a big role into looking the part.

For an extra push, a trainer can be a great way to get in shape. Not only will they push you harder than you would yourself, but you now have someone you are held accountable to. It is easy to eat that piece of cheesecake. It is harder to admit it to your trainer! It is important to have that love/hate relationship with your trainer; love the results/ hate the hard work!

Learn to Love A.M. Exercise

(Even if You're NOT A Morning Person)

I am not a morning person.

This confession will come as no surprise to my friends and family, most of whom have spent many glorious years making merry over my tendency to nod off over breakfast, my need for copious amounts of coffee before noon, and my late-night bursts of productivity.

For years I've tried to pretend I'm one of "them"—those chirpy, cheerful folks who rise effortlessly at dawn to go after that proverbial worm. I've also spent many years suppressing the urge to complain bitterly about a world where night owls like me suffer grievous discrimination at the hands of those ubiquitous "normal" people.

So those who know me best are always startled—no, make that shocked—to find out that I do most of my exercising in the early hours of the day, anywhere from 6 a.m. to 9 a.m. They're even more astonished, after an initial double take, to discover that I actually *like* to get my exercise in early.

Really.

And though my morning-exercise regimen started out as a concession to the practical constraints of my life, I have since discovered that there are some very good benefits to learning to love exercise in the morning—so I'll share with you my "**Top Ten Reasons**" **for getting up with the early birds to get moving**:

1. Exercising early in the morning "jump starts" your metabolism, keeping it elevated for hours, sometimes for up to 24 hours! As a result, you'll be burning more calories all day long—just because you exercised in the morning.

2. Exercising in the morning energizes you for the day—not to mention that gratifying feeling of virtue you have knowing you've done something disciplined *and* good for you. (Much better than a worm!)

3. Studies have shown that exercise significantly increases mental acuity—a benefit that lasts four to ten hours after your workout ends. Exercising in the a.m. means you get to harness that brainpower, instead of wasting it while you're snoozing.

4. Assuming you make exercise a true priority, it shouldn't be a major problem to get up 30 to 60 minutes earlier—especially since regular exercise generally means a higher quality of sleep, which in turn means you'll probably require less sleep. (If getting up 30 to 60 minutes earlier each day seems too daunting, you can ease into it with 10 to 20 minutes at first.)

5. When you exercise at about the same time every morning—especially if you wake up regularly at about the same time—you're regulating your body's endocrine system and circadian rhythms. Your body learns that you do the same thing just about every day, and it begins to prepare for waking and exercise several hours before you actually open your eyes. That's beneficial because:

- Your body's not "confused" by wildly changing wake-up times, which means waking up is much less painful. (You may even find that you don't need an alarm clock most days.)

- Hormones prepare your body for exercise by regulating blood pressure, heart rate, blood flow to muscles, etc.

- Your metabolism, along with all the hormones involved in activity and exercise, begin to elevate while you're sleeping. As a result, you'll feel more alert, energized, and ready to exercise when you do wake up.

- Many people find that morning exercise has a tendency to regulate their appetite for the rest of the day. Not only do they eat less (since activity causes the release of endorphins, which in turn diminishes appetite), they also choose healthier portions of healthier foods.

6. People who consistently exercise find, sometimes to their great surprise, that the appointed time every morning evolves into something they look forward to. Besides the satisfaction of taking care of themselves, they find it's a great time to plan their day, pray, or just think more clearly—things most of us often don't get to do otherwise.

7. Exercising first thing in the morning is the most foolproof way to ensure that other things don't overtake your fitness commitment, particularly if you have a hectic family life. (It's so easy to wimp out in the evening, when we're tired or faced with such tasks as rustling up dinner and helping with homework.)

8. More than 90% of those who exercise consistently have a morning fitness   routine. If you want to exercise on a regular basis, the odds are in your favor if you squeeze your workout into the a.m.

9. Non-morning people can always trick themselves in the a.m. Having trouble psyching yourself up for a sunrise jog? Do what I did—tell yourself that you'll still be so fast asleep that you won't even remember—much less mind!   [4]

---

[4] By Rebecca Pratt, Staff Writer for SparkPeople

Nutrition/ Diet

Your Diet Plan

You have to find what works for you and your body. The more natural the food, the better. For my body, I try to minimize my carbohydrates, especially right before I go to bed. If I eat bread, I make sure it is wheat bread. Your diet has a HUGE impact on how you look and feel.

Today, we have the advantage of free websites that will count your caloric intake. It is time to start thinking about the foods that you are putting in your mouth! Create a lifetime of healthy habits while you are young.

Just Remember: *Eating TOO few calories can make your body slow down it's metabolism by as* much *as 20%*. Biggest Loser

Alcohol & Weight Loss

Can You Have Both?

Alcohol and weight loss are enemies, but an occasional drink can have a place in a healthy lifestyle. In fact, many experts note the health benefits of consuming a single drink per day, including a reduced risk for high blood pressure. If, however, you are exceeding one drink daily, you might be sabotaging your weight loss plans.

Alcohol is metabolized differently than other foods and beverages. Under normal conditions, your body gets its energy from the calories in carbohydrates, fats and proteins that need to be slowly digested in the stomach—but not when alcohol is present. When alcohol is consumed, it gets special privileges and needs no digestion. The alcohol molecules diffuse through the stomach wall as soon as they arrive and can reach the brain and liver in minutes. This reaction is slightly slowed when there is also food in your system, but as soon as the mixed contents enter the small intestine, the alcohol grabs first place and is absorbed quickly. The alcohol then arrives at the liver for processing. The liver places all of its attention on the alcohol. Therefore, the carbohydrates (glucose) and dietary fats are just changed into body fat, waiting to be carried away for permanent fat storage in the body.

Alcohol is a diuretic, meaning that it causes water loss and dehydration. Along with this water loss you lose important minerals, such as magnesium, potassium, calcium and zinc. These minerals are vital to the maintenance of fluid balance, chemical reactions, and muscle contraction and relaxation.

Alcohol contains 7 calories per gram and offers NO nutritional value. It only adds empty calories to your diet. Why not spend your calorie budget on something healthier?

Alcohol affects your body in other negative ways.
Drinking might help induce sleep, but the sleep you get isn't very
deep. Ultimately, as a result, you get less rest. Alcohol can also
increase the amount of acid that your stomach produces, causing
your stomach lining to become inflamed. Over time, excessive
alcohol use can lead to serious health problems, including stomach
ulcers, liver disease, and heart troubles.

**Alcohol lowers your inhibitions, which is detrimental to
your diet plans.** Alcohol actually stimulates your appetite. While you
might be full from a comparable amount of calories from food,
several drinks might not fill you up. On top of that, research shows
that if you drink before or during a meal, both your inhibitions and
willpower are reduced. In this state, you are more likely to overeat—
especially greasy or fried foods—which can add to your waistline. To
avoid this, wait to order that drink until you're done with your meal.

Many foods that accompany drinking (peanuts, pretzels,
chips) are salty, which can make you thirsty, encouraging you to drink
even more. To avoid overdrinking, sip on a glass of water in between
each alcoholic beverage.

**Skipping a meal to save your calories for drinks later is a
bad idea.** Many drinkers know they'll be having some alcohol later,
whether going to a bar, party, or just kicking back at home. Knowing

that drinking entails extra calories, it may be tempting to "bank" some calories by skipping a meal or two. This is a bad move. If you come to the bar hungry, you are even more likely to munch on the snacks, and drinking on an empty stomach enhances the negative effects of alcohol. If you're planning on drinking later, eat a healthy meal first. You'll feel fuller, which will stop you from overdrinking. If you are worried about a looming night out with friends, include an extra 30 minutes of exercise to balance your calories—instead of skipping a meal.

What are more important, calories or carbs? You might think that drinking liquor is more diet-friendly because it has no carbohydrates, while both wine and beer do contain carbs. But dieters need to watch calories, and liquor only has a few calories less than beer or wine. Plus, it is often mixed with other drinks, adding even more empty calories. Hard liquor contains around 100 calories per shot, so adding a mixer increases calories even more. If you are going to mix liquor with anything, opt for a diet or club soda, instead of fruit juice or regular soda. Sweeter drinks, whether liquor or wine, tend to have more sugar, and therefore more calories. In that respect, dry wines usually have fewer calories than sweet wines.

The list below breaks down the number of calories in typical alcoholic drinks. Compare some of your favorites to make a good choice next time you decide to indulge in a serving of alcohol. [5]

Drink	Serving Size	Calories
Red wine	5 oz.	100
White wine	5 oz.	100
Champagne	5 oz.	130
Light beer	12 oz.	105
Regular beer	12 oz.	140
Dark beer	12 oz.	170
Cosmopolitan	3 oz.	165
Martini	3 oz.	205
Long Island iced tea	8 oz.	400
Gin & Tonic	8 oz.	175
Rum & Soda	8 oz.	180
Margarita	8 oz.	200
Whiskey Sour	4 oz.	200

[5] *By Liz Noelcke, Staff Writer for SparkPeople*

How to Look Thinner Instantly!

Good carriage not only conveys confidence and poise- it can give you a slimmer looking body. "Proper posture elongates the neck and torso, making you seem leaner, even taller," says Julie Kent, a principle dancer with American Ballet Theatre in New York City.

- Hold your neck straight to give yourself a taller, more graceful look.
- Keep your shoulders down and squared to create an air of confidence.
- Let your arms hang straight down (slightly away from your torso) to make your waist seem slimmer.
- Lift your rib cage up toward the ceiling, allowing your midsection to appear trim and toned.
- Contract your abdominals slightly- results in a sleeker look and a firmer tummy.
- Gently tuck your buttocks under to elongate your torso.
- Keep your knees straight, not locked, to assure that you stand your tallest.
- Place your feet hip-distance apart and parallel, with your weight evenly balanced, to make you look poised.[6]

---

[6] *McCall's October 1995*

Hair & Make-Up

The key to hair and make-up is to look glamorous and not to overdo it. Extreme and severe looks are discouraged among most teams. You want to look as natural as possible, with a little enhancing. Studying the hair and make-up of the current team will help you tremendously.

Keeping your hair out of your face during the audition is a must. Practice dancing with your hair down; i.e. no ponytails, etc. If you make the squad, you will need to be able to maintain a beautiful look throughout a 3 hour game. Be familiar with products that will hold your hair. Many squads have a preferred salon, so advice can always be given by the people behind the scenes. If you use extensions or hair pieces, make sure they a natural looking and secured!

For make-up, natural tones can avoid a harsh look. Enhance the eyes with eye lashes and eye liner- just don't go overboard! Make sure you have lip color that is seen from a distance and that can withhold a long period of time.

Take care of your hands! It may seem like a small detail, but it can be the first thing that people notice. Natural and French manicures are professional and do not compete with your audition attire.

Once you make a squad, the director/ staff may advise you to make changes (i.e. hair color, make-up technique, etc.). Be prepared and trust that they know what they are doing! Part of a director's job is to make sure all of the women have a polished look.

Know the Rules of the Game

Football 101

The Field

Learning the exact dimensions of the field is not necessarily that important, but it is good to have a basic knowledge of the field itself. You'll notice from this illustration: (right click on the link to open in a new window)

- The playing field is 100 yards long.
- It has stripes running across the field at five-yard intervals.
- There are shorter lines, called hash marks, marking each one-yard interval. (not shown)
- On each end of the playing field is an end zone (red section with diagonal lines) which extends ten yards.
- The total field is 120 yards long and 160 feet wide.

The Game

Each team is comprised of an offense, defense, and special teams.

- Each game features two teams playing against each other.
- Each team is allowed 11 men on the field at a time. Any more than 11 could result in a penalty.
- Unlimited substitution is permitted, but players may only enter the field when the ball is dead.
- Each team is comprised of an offense, defense, and special teams.
- If team A has possession of the ball, they use their offensive team to attempt to advance the ball toward the opponent's endzone.
- If team B has the ball, team A will use their defensive team to attempt to stop team B from advancing the ball.
- If a kicking play is expected, both teams will use their special teams.

Object of the Game

- The object of the game is to outscore your opponent by advancing the football into their endzone for as many touchdowns as possible while holding them to as few as possible. There are other ways of scoring, but a touchdown is usually the prime objective.

Beginning of the Game

• Before each game, the captains from each team and the referee meet at the center of the field for the coin toss.

• The winner of the coin toss has the option of starting the game by kicking the ball to the other team or receiving the kickoff from the other team.

• The game begins when one of the teams kicks off to the other.

• The receiving team must catch the ball and try to advance it as far back toward the kicking team as possible.

• The play ends when the player with the ball is knocked to the ground (tackled), or makes it all the way to the kicking team's endzone (touchdown).

• The spot where the kick returner was tackled becomes the line of scrimmage. The line of scrimmage is a term for the place the ball is spotted before a play is run.

• Once this starting point is established, the offensive squad of the receiving team will come in and try to move the ball toward the opposition's end zone.

Down & Distance

Understanding down and distance is probably the biggest key to understanding football, so make sure you really understand this part before moving on to the next section.

• Basically, a down is a play. From the time the ball is snapped (put into play), to the time the play is whistled over by the officials, is considered one down.

• A team's offense is given four downs (plays) to move ten yards toward the opponent's end zone.

• Distance is the number of yards a team needs to get a new set of four downs.

• If they make the ten yards needed within four downs, they are given a new set of downs. This is called getting a first down.

• If they don't make it the required ten yards, the other team's offense takes possession of the ball.

An Example

• The first play of a series is called first-and-ten because it is the first down and ten yards are needed to receive a new set of four downs.

• Suppose on the first play, the team on offense picks up three yards. The next play would then be second-and-seven, because it is the second play of the set and they still need seven yards to get a first down.

• If they were to pick up six yards on the second play it would leave them one yard shy of the first down marker, therefore setting up a third-and-one situation. Third-and-one because it would be the third play of the series and they would still need one yard to get a first down.

- If the team with the ball can pick up one yard or more on the third-down play, then they will be given a first down, which means they get to start all over with a new set of four downs.
- A team can continue moving the football down the field as long as they continue to pick up first downs.

Fourth-Down Strategies

If a team fails to gain the required yardage on third down, several things could happen on fourth down:

- A team can elect to "go for it" on fourth down and try to pick up the remaining yardage, but they run the risk of turning the ball over to the other team if they do not get to the first down marker. If they do not get the required yardage, the other team takes possession of the ball at the spot of the last tackle and now has four downs to move ten yards back in the other direction.
- The majority of the time, teams will elect to "punt" the ball away on fourth down. A punt is simply a form of kicking the ball that gives possession of the ball to the other team, but also pushes them back considerably farther away from the end zone.
- Another option is to kick a field goal. If a team feels they are close enough to kick the ball between the upright bars of the goal post in their opponent's endzone, they may attempt a field goal, which is worth three points when converted successfully.

After a Score

• After a team scores via a touchdown or field goal, they must, in turn, kick off to the other team, and the process begins all over again.

Methods of Scoring

• The biggest goal for an offense, every time they take possession of the ball, is to score a touchdown. To score a touchdown, a player must carry the ball across the opposition's goal line, or catch a pass in the end zone. Once the ball crosses the plane of the goal line while it is in a player's possession, it is scored a touchdown. A touchdown is worth six points.

• The team scoring a touchdown is given the bonus of trying to add one or two more points. These are called extra point conversion attempts.

• If a team elects to go for two extra points, they will line up at the two-yard line and make one attempt at either running or passing the ball into the end zone. If they make it, they are awarded two points. If they don't, they get no extra points.

• They can also elect to go for just one extra point by kicking the ball through the goal posts from the two-yard line.

• Another way for a team to score is by kicking a field goal. When a team finds themselves in a fourth-down situation, many times they will attempt to kick a field goal if they feel they are close enough for their kicker to kick the football between the upright bars of the goal post in the opponent's endzone. A field goal is worth three points.

• A team can also pick up two points by tackling an opponent possessing the ball in their own end zone. This is called a safety!

Perhaps the rarest way to score in football is on the little-used fair-catch kick. If a team fair catches a punt from the other team, they have the option of attempting a field goal on a free kick on the very next play from the spot the punt is fielded. The ball is kicked off the ground with the aid of a holder, and is worth three points just like a regular field goal. The down is not timed.

To summarize:
Touchdown = 6 points
Extra Point Conversion = 1 point
Two-Point Conversion = 2 points
Field Goal = 3 points
Safety= 2 points

Basic Positions on Offense

Quarterback

The player who receives the ball from the center at the start of each play before either handing it to the running back, throwing it to a receiver, or running with it himself.

The quarterback is usually the player in charge of running the offense on the field. He is also the guy that usually informs the offense of the play while in the huddle.

Halfback

An offensive player who lines up in the backfield and generally is responsible for carrying the ball on run plays. A running back's primary role is to run with the football, he is also used as a receiver at times.

Fullback

An offensive player who lines up in the offensive backfield and generally is responsible for run-blocking for the halfback and pass-blocking for the quarterback. Fullbacks are usually bigger than halfbacks, and also serve as short-yardage runners.

Wide Receiver

An offensive player who lines up on or near the line of scrimmage, but split to the outside. His primary job is to catch passes from the quarterback.

Tight End

An offensive player who serves as a receiver and also a blocker. The tight end lines up beside the offensive tackle either to the right or to the left of the quarterback.

Offensive Tackle

A member of the offensive line. There are two tackles on every play, and they line up on the outside of the offensive guards.

Offensive Guard A member of the offensive line. There are two guards on every play, and they line up on either side of the offensive center.

Center The offensive lineman who hikes (or snaps) the ball to the quarterback at the start of each play. The center lines up in the middle of the offensive line, between the offensive guards.

Basic Positions on Defense

Defensive End

A defensive player who lines up at the end of the defensive line. The job of the defensive end is to contain the running back on running plays to the outside, and rush the quarterback on passing plays.

Defensive Tackle

A defensive player who lines up on the interior of the defensive line.

The duties of a defensive tackle include stopping the running back on running plays, getting pressure up the middle on passing plays, and occupying blockers so the linebackers can roam free.

Nose Tackle

The defensive player who lines up directly across from the center. Also known as:the nose guard, the primary responsibilities of the nose tackle are to stop the run and occupy the offensive lineman to keep them from blocking the linebackers.

Linebacker

A defensive player who lines up behind the defensive linemen and in front of the defensive backfield. The linebackers are a team's second line of defense. Each team has two outside linebackers. In a 4-3 defense, teams have one inside linebacker, usually referred to as a middle linebacker. In a 3-4 defense teams have two inside linebackers.

Cornerback

A defensive back who generally lines up on the outside of the formation and is usually assigned to cover a wide receiver.

Safety

A defensive back who lines up in the secondary between, but generally deeper than the cornerbacks. His primary duties include helping the cornerbacks in pass coverage. There are actually two safety positions; the free safety and the strong safety.

Positions on Special Teams

*These definitions cover the specialized positions on special teams only.

Gunner

The members of the special teams who specialize in racing downfield to tackle the kick or punt returner. The gunners usually line up on the outside of the offensive line and are often double teamed by blockers.

Holder

The player who catches the snap from the center and places it down for the placekicker to attempt to kick it through the uprights of the goalpost. On an attempted field goal, the holder must catch the ball and put it into a good kicking position, ideally with the laces facing away from the kicker.

Kick Returner

A kick returner is the player that catches kickoffs and attempts to return them in the opposite direction. He is usually one of the faster players on the team, often a reserve wide receiver.

Long Snapper

The center position as it would be played on offense, but this player specializes in making longer snaps for punts and field goal attempts. A long-snapper generally has to snap the ball seven-to-eight yards behind him for field goal attempts and 13 to 15 yards for punts with the accuracy that allows the holder or punter to handle the ball cleanly.

Placekicker

The player who kicks the ball on kickoffs, extra point attempts, and field goal attempts. A placekicker either kicks the ball while it's being held by a teammate or kicks it off a tee.

Punter

The player who stands behind the line of scrimmage, catches the long snap from the center, and then kicks the ball after dropping it toward his foot. The punter generally comes in on fourth down to punt the ball to the other team with the idea of driving the other team as far back as possible before they take possession of the ball.

Punt Returner

The job of a punt returner is to catch the ball after it has been punted and run it back toward the punting team's end zone.

Officials & Their Signals

In the NFL, there are seven officials:

Referee: The head of the team, he is the one you see on TV, he is in control of the game, gives signals and is the final authority. He lines up behind the offense 10-12 yards, watches the snap, motion, blocks and passes. Sets final position of the ball at the end of the play.

Umpire: Lines up 4-5 yards behind the defensive line, watches blocking, players equipment, player conduct and actions at the line of scrimmage.

Head Linesman: Lines up outside the offensive formation at the line of scrimmage (to the quarterback's right side) watches for off-sides, encroachment, etc. Rules on out of bounds on his side of the field. Helps the Referee with the final spot of the ball and rules on pass completions.

Line Judge: Lines up outside the offensive formation at the line of scrimmage (to the quarterback's left side) watches for off-sides, encroachment, etc. Rules on out of bounds on his side of the field. Watches anything that happens on the Umpire's blind side.

Back Judge: Lines up 17 yards downfield of the Line Judge. He watches the receivers on his side of the field, makes rulings on down field blocks, catches, illegal touching, interceptions, pass interference and down field loose balls.

Side Judge: Lines up 17 yards downfield of the Head Linesman. He watches the receivers on his side of the field, makes rulings on down field blocks, catches, illegal touching, interceptions, pass interference and down field loose balls.

Field Judge: Lines up 25 yards downfield (in the center of the field). He watches the tight end, runs the play clock, makes rulings on down field blocks, catches, illegal touching, interceptions, pass interference and down field loose balls.[7]

---

[7] James Alder, About.com Guide

Basketball 101

Definitions

Section I-Basket/Backboard

a. A team's basket consists of the basket ring and net through which its players try to shoot the ball. The visiting team has the choice of baskets for the first half. The basket selected by the visiting team when it first enters onto the court shall be its basket for the first half.

b. The teams change baskets for the second half. All overtime periods are considered extensions of the second half.

c. Five sides of the backboard (front, two sides, bottom and top) are considered in play when contacted by the basketball. The back of the backboard and the area directly behind it are out-of-bounds.

Section II-Blocking

Blocking is illegal personal contact which impedes the progress of an opponent.

1) ### Section III-Dribble

A dribble is movement of the ball, caused by a player in control, who throws or taps the ball into the air or to the floor.

a. The dribble ends when the dribbler:

(1) Touches the ball simultaneously with both hands

(2) Permits the ball to come to rest while he is in control of it

(3) Tries for a field goal

(4) Throws a pass

(5) Touches the ball more than once while dribbling, before it touches the floor

(6) Loses control

(7) Allows the ball to become dead

Section IV-Fouls

a. A common personal foul is illegal physical contact which occurs with an opponent after the ball has become live.

b. A technical foul is the penalty for unsportsmanlike conduct or violations by team members on the floor or seated on the bench. It may be assessed for illegal contact which occurs with an opponent before the ball becomes live.

c. A double foul is a situation in which two opponents commit personal or technical fouls against each other at approximately the same time.

d. An offensive foul is illegal contact, committed by an offensive player, after the ball is live.

e. A loose ball foul is illegal contact, after the ball is alive, when team control does not exist.

f. An elbow foul is making contact with the elbow in an unsportsmanlike manner whether the ball is dead or alive.

g. A flagrant foul is unnecessary and/or excessive contact committed by a player against an opponent whether the ball is dead or alive.

h. A punching foul is a punch by a player which makes contact with an opponent whether the ball is dead or alive.

i. An away-from-the-play foul is illegal contact by the defense in the last two minutes of the game, and/or overtime, which occurs (1) deliberately away from the immediate area of offensive action, and/or (2) prior to the ball being released on a throw-in.

Section V-Free Throw

A free throw is the privilege given a player to score one point by an unhindered attempt for the goal from a position directly behind the free throw line. This attempt must be made within 10 seconds.

Section VI-Frontcourt/Backcourt

a. A team's frontcourt consists of that part of the court between its endline and the nearer edge of the midcourt line, including the basket and inbounds part of the backboard.

b. A team's backcourt consists of the entire midcourt line and the rest of the court to include the opponent's basket and inbounds part of the backboard.

c. A ball being held by a player: (1) is in the frontcourt if neither the ball nor the player is touching the backcourt, (2) is in the backcourt if either the ball or player is touching the backcourt.

d. A ball being dribbled is (1) in the frontcourt when the ball and both feet of the player are in the frontcourt, (2) in the backcourt if the ball or either foot of the player is in the backcourt.

e. The ball is considered in the frontcourt once it has broken the plane of the midcourt line and is not in player control.

f. The team on offense must bring the ball across the midcourt line within 8 seconds. No additional 10-second count is permitted in the backcourt.

EXCEPTION: (1) kicked ball, (2) punched ball, (3) technical foul on the defensive team, (4) delay-of-game warning on the defensive team or (5) infection control.

g. Frontcourt/backcourt status is not attained until a player with the ball has established a positive position in either half during (1) a jump ball, (2) a steal by a defensive player, or (3) a throw-in in the last two minutes of the fourth period and/or any overtime period.

Section VII-Held Ball

A held ball occurs when two opponents have one or both hands firmly on the ball. A held ball should not be called until both players have hands so firmly on the ball that neither can gain sole possession without undue roughness. If a player is lying or sitting on the floor while in possession, he should have an opportunity to throw the ball, but a held ball should be called if there is danger of injury.

Section VIII-Pivot

a. A pivot takes place when a player, who is holding the ball, steps once or more than once in any direction with the same foot, with the other foot (pivot foot) in contact with the floor.

b. If the player wishes to dribble after a pivot, the ball must be out of his hand before the pivot foot is raised off the floor. If the player raises his pivot off the floor, he must pass or attempt a field goal. If he fails to follow these guidelines, he has committed a traveling violation.

Section IX-Traveling

Traveling is progressing in any direction while in possession of the ball, which is in excess of prescribed limits as noted in Rule 4- Section VIII and Rule 10- Section XIV.

Section X-Screen

A screen is the legal action of a player who, without causing undue contact, delays or prevents an opponent from reaching a desired position.

Section XI-Field Goal Attempt

A field goal attempt is a player's attempt to shoot the ball into his basket for a field goal. The act of shooting starts when, in the official's judgment, the player has started his shooting motion and continues until the shooting motion ceases and he returns to a normal floor position. It is not essential that the ball leave the shooter's hand. His arm(s) might be held so that he cannot actually make an attempt. The term is also used to include the flight of the ball until it becomes dead or is touched by a player. A tap during a jump ball or rebound is not considered a field goal attempt. However, anytime a live ball is in flight from the playing court, the goal, if made, shall count, even if time expires or the official's whistle sounds. The field goal will not be scored if time on the game clock expires before the ball leaves the player's hand.

Section XII-Throw-In

A throw-in is a method of putting the ball in play from out-of-bounds in accordance with Rule 8-Section III. The throw-in begins when the ball is at the disposal of the team or player entitled to it, and ends when the ball is released by the thrower-in.

Section XIII-Last Two Minutes

When the game clock shows 2:00, the game is considered to be in the two-minute period.

Section XIV-Disconcertion of Free Throw Shooter

Disconcertion of the free throw shooter is any of the following:

a. During multiple free throw attempts which are not going to remain in play, an opponent may not, while located on the lane lines, be allowed to raise his arms above his head.

b. During any free throw attempt, an opponent in the game who is in the visual field of the free throw shooter, may not (1) wave his arms, (2) make a sudden dash upcourt, (3) talk to the free throw shooter, or (4) talk loudly in a disruptive manner.

Section XV-Suspension of Play

An official can suspend play for retrieving an errant ball, re-setting the timing devices, delay-of-game warning, inadvertent whistle or any other unusual circumstance. During such a suspension, neither team is permitted to substitute and only the offensive team can request a timeout. Play shall be resumed at the point of interruption.

Section XVI-Point of Interruption

Where the ball is located when the whistle sounds.

Section XVII-Team Control

A team is in control when a player is holding, dribbling or passing the ball. Team control ends when the defensive team deflects the ball or there is a field goal attempt.

Section XVIII-Team Possession

A team is in possession when a player is holding, dribbling or passing the ball. Team possession ends when the defensive team gains possession or there is a field goal attempt.

Players, Substitutions, & Coaches

Section I-Team

a. Each team shall consist of five players. No team may be reduced to less than five players. If a player in the game receives his sixth personal foul and all substitutes have already been disqualified, said player shall remain in the game and shall be charged with a personal and team foul. A technical foul also shall be assessed against his team. All subsequent personal fouls, including offensive fouls, shall be treated similarly. All players who have six or more personal fouls and remain in the game shall be treated similarly.

b. In the event that there are only five eligible players remaining and one of these players is injured and must leave the game or is ejected, he must be replaced by the last player who was disqualified by reason of receiving six personal fouls. Each subsequent requirement to replace an injured or ejected player will be treated in this inverse order. Any such re-entry into a game by a disqualified player shall be penalized by a technical foul.

c. In the event that a player becomes ill and must leave the court while the ball is in play, the official will stop play immediately when his team gains new possession. The player shall be replaced and no technical foul will be assessed. The opposing team is also permitted to substitute one player.

Section II-Starting Line-Ups

At least ten minutes before the game is scheduled to begin, the scorers shall be supplied with the name and number of each player who may participate in the game. Starting line-ups will be indicated. Failure to comply with this provision shall be reported to the Basketball Operations Department.

Section III-The Captain

a. A team may have a captain and a co-captain numbering a maximum of two. The designated captain may be anyone on the squad who is in uniform, except a player-coach.

b. The designated captain is the only player who may ask an official about a rule interpretation during a regular or 20-second timeout charged to his team. He may not discuss a judgment decision.

c. If the designated captain continues to sit on the bench, he remains the captain for the entire game.

d. In the event that the captain is absent from the court and bench, his coach shall immediately designate a new captain.

Section IV-The Coach and Others

a. The coach's position may be on or off the bench from the 28' hash mark to the baseline. They are permitted between the 28' hash mark and the midcourt line to relay information to players but must return to the bench side of the 28' hash mark immediately or be called for an non-unsportsmanlike technical foul. A coach is not permitted to cross the midcourt line and violators will be assessed an unsportsmanlike technical foul immediately. All assistants and trainers must remain on the bench. Coaches and trainers are not permitted to go to the scorer's table, for any reason, except during a deadball.

b. A player-coach will have no special privileges. He is to conduct himself in the same manner as any other player.

c. Any club personnel not seated on the bench must conduct themselves in a manner that would reflect favorably on the dignity of the game or that of the officials. Violations by any of the personnel indicated shall require a written report to the Basketball Operations Department for subsequent action.

d. The bench shall be occupied only by a league-approved head coach, a maximum of three assistant coaches, players and trainer. During an altercation, the head and assistant coaches are permitted on the court.

Scoring & Timing

Section I-Scoring

a. A legal field goal or free throw attempt shall be scored when a live ball from the playing area enters the basket from above and remains in or passes through the net.

b. A successful field goal attempt from the area on or inside the three-point field goal line shall count two points.

c. A successful field goal attempt from the area outside the three-point field goal line shall count three points.

(1) The shooter must have at least one foot on the floor outside the three-point field goal line prior to the attempt.

(2) The shooter may not be touching the floor on or inside the three-point field goal line.

(3) The shooter may contact the three-point field goal line, or land in the two-point field goal area, after the ball is released.

d. A field goal accidentally scored in an opponent's basket shall be added to the opponent's score, credited to the opposing player nearest the shooter and mentioned in a footnote.

e. It is a violation for a player to attempt a field goal at an opponent's basket. The opposing team will be awarded the ball at the free throw line extended.

f. A successful free throw attempt shall count one point.

g. An unsuccessful free throw attempt which is tapped into the basket shall count two points and shall be credited to the player who tapped the ball in.

h. If there is a discrepancy in the score and it cannot be resolved, the running score shall be official.

Section II-Timing

a. All periods of regulation play in the NBA will be twelve minutes.

b. All overtime periods of play will be five minutes.

c. Fifteen minutes will be permitted between halves of all games.

d. 130 seconds will be permitted between the first and second periods, the third and fourth periods and before any overtime period.

e. A team is permitted 30 seconds to replace a disqualified player.

f. The game is considered to be in the two-minute part when the game clock shows 2:00 or less time remaining in the period.

g. The public address operator is required to announce that there are two minutes remaining in each period.

h. The game clock shall be equipped to show tenths-of-a-second during the last minute of each period.

Section III-End of Period

a. Each period ends when time expires.

EXCEPTIONS:

(1) If a live ball is in flight, the period ends when the goal is made, missed or touched by an offensive player.

(2) If the official's whistle sounds prior to the horn or :00.0 on the clock, the period is not over and time must be added to the clock.

(3) If the ball is in the air when the horn sounds ending a period, and it subsequently is touched by: (a) a defensive player, the goal, if successful, shall count; or (b) an offensive player, the period has ended.

(4) If a timeout request is made at approximately the instant time expires for a period, the period ends and the timeout shall not be granted.

b. If the ball is dead and the game clock shows :00.0, the period has ended even though the horn may not have sounded.

Section IV-Tie Score-Overtime

If the score is tied at the end of the fourth period, play shall resume in 130 seconds without change of baskets for any of the overtime periods required. (See Rule 5-Section II-d for the amount of time between overtime periods.)

Section V-Stoppage of Timing Devices

a. The timing devices shall be stopped whenever the official's whistle sounds indicating one of the following:

(1) A personal or technical foul.

(2) A jump ball.

(3) A floor violation.

(4) An unusual delay.

(5) A suspension-of-play for any other emergency (no substitutions are permitted.)

(6) A regular or 20-second timeout.

b. The timing devices shall be stopped:

(1) During the last minute of the first, second and third periods following a successful field goal attempt.

(2)During the last two minutes of regulation play and/or overtime(s) following a successful field goal attempt.

c. Officials may not use official time to permit a player to change or repair equipment.

Section VI-20-Second Timeout

A player's request for a 20-second timeout shall be granted only when the ball is dead or in control of the team making the request. A request at any other time shall be ignored.

EXCEPTION: The head coach may request a 20-second timeout

if there is a suspension of play to administer Comments on the Rules-N-Guidelines for Infection Control.

a. Each team is entitled to one (1) 20-second timeout per half for a total of two (2) per game, including overtimes.

b. During a 20-second timeout a team may only substitute for one player. If the team calling the 20-second timeout replaces a player, the opposing team may also replace one player. EXCEPTION: In the last two minutes of the fourth period and/or any overtime period, free substitution is permitted by both teams.

c. If a second 20-second timeout is requested during a half (including over-times), it shall be granted. It will automatically become a charged regular timeout. Overtimes are considered to be an extension of the second half.

d. The official shall instruct the timer to record the 20 seconds and to inform him when the time has expired. An additional regular timeout will be charged if play is unable to resume at the expiration of that 20-second time limit. EXCEPTION: No regular timeout remaining and an injured player on the court.

e. This rule may be used for any reason, including a request for a rule interpretation. If the correction is sustained, no timeout shall be charged.

f. Players should say "20-second timeout" when requesting this time.

g. If a 20-second timeout is requested by the offensive team during the last two minutes of the fourth period and/or any overtime period and (1) the ball is out-of-bounds in the backcourt (except for a suspension of play), or (2) after securing the ball from a rebound and prior to any advance of the ball, or (3) after the offensive team secures the ball from a change of possession and prior to any advance of the ball, the timeout should be granted. Upon resumption of play, the team granted the timeout shall have the option of putting the ball into play at the 28' hash mark in the frontcourt or at the designated spot out-of-bounds. If the ball is put into play at the hash mark, the ball may be passed into either the frontcourt or backcourt. If it is passed into the backcourt, the team will receive a new 8-second count.

h. If a 20-second timeout has been granted and a mandatory timeout by the same team is due, only the mandatory timeout will be charged.

i. A 20-second timeout shall not be granted to the defensive team during an official's suspension-of-play for (1) delay-of-game warning, (2) retrieving an errant ball, (3) an inadvertent whistle or (4) any other unusual circumstance.

EXCEPTION: Suspension of play for a player bleeding. See Comments on the Rules-N.

Section VII-Regular Timeout-100/60 Seconds

A player's request for a timeout shall be granted only when the ball is dead or in control of the team making the request. A request at any other time shall be ignored.

EXCEPTION: The head coach may request a regular timeout if there is a suspension of play to administer Comments on the Rules-N-Guidelines for Infection Control.

> a. Each team is entitled to six (6) charged timeouts during regulation play. Each team is limited to no more than three (3) timeouts in the fourth period and no more than two (2) timeouts in the last two minutes of regulation play. (This is in addition to one 20-second timeout per half.)
> b. During a regular timeout, both teams may have unlimited substitutions.

> c. In overtime periods each team shall be allowed three (3) 60-second timeouts regardless of the number of timeouts called or remaining during regulation play or previous overtimes. Teams are permitted no more than two timeouts in the last two minutes of the period.
> d. There must be two 100-second timeouts in the first and third periods and three 100-second timeouts in the second and fourth periods. If neither team has taken a timeout prior to 5:59 of the first or third period, it shall be mandatory for the Official Scorer to take it at the first dead ball and charge it to the home team. If no subsequent timeouts are taken prior

to 2:59, it shall be mandatory for the Official Scorer to take it and charge it to the team not previously charged. If neither team has taken a timeout prior to 8:59 of the second or fourth period, a mandatory timeout will be called by the Official Scorer and charged to neither team. If there are no subsequent timeouts taken prior to 5:59, it shall be mandatory for the Official Scorer to take it at the first dead ball and charge it to the home team. If no subsequent timeouts are taken prior to 2:59, it shall be mandatory for the Official Scorer to take it and charge it to the team not previously charged. The Official Scorer shall notify a team when it has been charged with a mandatory timeout. Any additional timeouts in a period beyond those which are mandatory shall be 60 seconds. No regular or mandatory timeout shall be granted to the defensive team during an official's suspension-of-play for (1) a delay-of-game warning, (2) retrieving an errant ball, (3) an inadvertent whistle, or (4) any other unusual circumstance.

EXCEPTION: Suspension-of-play for Infection Control. See Comments on the Rules-N.

e. If a regular or mandatory timeout is awarded the offensive team during the last two minutes of the fourth period and/or any overtime period and (1) the ball is out-of-bounds in the backcourt (except for a suspension of play), or (2) after securing the ball from a rebound and prior to any advance of the ball, or (3) after securing the ball from a change of possession and prior to any advance of the ball, the timeout shall be granted. Upon resumption of play, the team granted the timeout shall have the option of putting the ball into play at the 28' hash mark in the frontcourt, or at the designated spot out-of-bounds. If the ball is put into play at the hash mark, the ball may be passed into either the frontcourt or backcourt. If the ball is passed into the backcourt, the team will receive a new 8-second count. However, once the ball is (1) thrown in from out-of-bounds, or (2) dribbled or passed after receiving it from a rebound or a change of possession, the timeout shall be granted, and, upon resumption of play, the ball shall be in-bounded on the side- line where play was interrupted. The time on the game clock and the 24-second clock shall remain as when the timeout was called. In order for the option to be available under the conditions in paragraph #2 above, the offensive team must call two successive timeouts.

f. No timeout shall be charged if it is called to question a rule interpretation and the correction is sustained.

g. Requests for a timeout in excess of the authorized number shall be granted and a technical foul shall be assessed. Following the timeout, the ball will be awarded to the opposing team and play shall resume with a throw-in nearest the spot where play was interrupted.

Section VIII-Timeout Requests

a. If an official, upon receiving a timeout request (regular or 20-second) by the defensive team, inadvertently signals while the play is in progress, play shall be suspended and the team in possession shall put the ball in play immediately at the sideline nearest where the ball was when the signal was given. The team in possession shall have only the time remaining of the original eight seconds in which to move the ball into the frontcourt. The 24-second clock shall remain the same.

b. If an official, upon receiving a timeout request (regular or 20-second) from the defensive team, inadvertently signals for a timeout during: (1) a successful field goal or free throw attempt, the point(s) shall be scored; (2) an unsuccessful field goal attempt, play shall be resumed with a jump ball at the center circle between any two opponents; (3) an unsuccessful free throw attempt, the official shall rule disconcerting and award a substitute free throw.

c. If an official inadvertently blows his whistle during (1) a successful field goal or free throw attempt, the points shall be scored, or (2) an unsuccessful field goal or free throw attempt, play shall be resumed with a jump ball at the center circle between any two opponents.

d. When a team is granted a regular or 20-second time-out, play shall not resume until the full 100 seconds, 60 seconds, or 20 seconds have elapsed. The throw-in shall be nearest the spot where play was suspended. The throw-in shall be on the sideline, if the ball was in play when the request was granted.

e. A player shall not be granted a timeout (regular or 20-second) if both of his feet are in the air and any part of his body has broken the vertical plane of the boundary line (including the midcourt line).

Section IX-Time-In

a. After time has been out, the game clock shall be started when the ball is legally touched by any player within the playing area of the court.

b. On a free throw that is unsuccessful and the ball continues in play, the game clock shall be started when the missed free throw is legally touched by any player.

c. If play is resumed by a throw-in from out-of-bounds, the game clock shall be started when the ball is legally touched by any player within the playing area of the court.

d. If play is resumed with a jump ball, the game clock shall be started when the ball is legally tapped. [8]

---

[8] Provided by www. nba.com

Chapter 5

Politics

Some luck lies in not getting what you wanted but getting what you have, which once you have got it you might be smart enough to see is what you would have wanted had you known."

Garrison Keillor

As with any job, politics can play a role into which dancers are picked. It can happen on the college level, as well as the professional. My best advice for that is to do the best you can to beat out the politics. It is unfair and happens in *every* arena in life. However, I have seen talent out beat so-and-so's sister. You can only do what you can. Eventually, fate steps in, and if you were meant to make it, you will. Stressing out about it will <u>not</u> help the situation and can lead to bitterness. There will always be a member or two that you feel should not have made it. They may not have the same level of talent as the rest of the squad. The unique view of this, however, is that they may have been chosen to be on the squad for reasons unknown to anyone but the director. Perhaps they have great communication skills and would represent the squad well at appearances. Or they have potential to be great, but have not been given the appropriate training. Whatever the reason, the wise and mature attitude to have is to trust the decisions that are made. I am not saying that you have to agree with the decision, but instead, show respect.

"I can't change the direction of the wind, but I can adjust my sails to always reach my destination." -- Jimmy Dean, Actor, Singer and Businessman

Chapter 6

The Experience

"That it will never come again is what makes life so sweet."

Emily Dickenson

Is it worth it? All of the stress, evaluation, overbooked schedule, etc., etc. I can, without a doubt, answer that question by saying yes! There are so many opportunities to be earned just by making a team. You may have the opportunity to perform in foreign countries , meet celebrities, and give back to the community you serve.

There are, of course, many sacrifices you will have to make. Your relationships will begin to take a toll. Friends or boyfriends may not adapt too well to having to be penciled in- just in case you have a last minute appearance! You will have to become a professional at managing your time/schedule.

Performing in front of thousands of fans is the biggest rush I have ever had in my life. With arenas holding up to 90,000 fans, there is always a pair of eyes watching your performance. The pressure forces you to perform to the best of your ability. It is your moment to shine and capture in your memory for a lifetime. Practicing long strenuous hours all pays off in a matter of a few minutes on the court or field.

"Occasionally in life there are those moments of unutterable fulfillment which cannot be completely explained by those symbols called words. Their meanings can only be articulated by the inaudible language of the heart."

Dr. Martin Luther King, Jr.

Other opportunities include charity appearances, being published in calendars and magazines, and flying overseas to entertain the troops. The possibilities are endless, and there are more now than when I began.

Chapter 7

Never Give Up, Never Surrender

One day in retrospect, the years of struggle will strike you as the most beautiful."

Sigmund Freud

As you begin the tryout process, you will realize that some of the girls that you are trying out with have tried out before. It is somewhat difficult to make an established squad the very first time you tryout. Please do not misunderstand me. I am not saying it is impossible. I have, however, met several women that tried out for the same squad 5, 6, and 7 years before actually making the squad.

The main thing to ask yourself is how badly do you want it? Are you willing to keep trying out, regardless of the outcome? To take away from each audition constructive criticism to make yourself a better dancer and performer?

The key to each successful and a not so successful audition is to be a good sport. I can remember girls just bawling their eyes out when they found out they did not make the team. I never wanted to be <u>THAT</u> girl. Many directors remember how you handled the stress of not making the squad the next year you try out. Composure is the key. If you feel the need to cry, do it in the comfort of your own home! Then pick yourself up, train some more, and create a better you!

"I do not try to dance better than anyone else...
I only try to dance better than myself."
Mikhail Baryshnikov

You are in the midst of creating character. How you react to success or defeat can affect every aspect of your life. Only a handful of ladies can make it, but you can take away from it what you put into it. Making friends, improving technique, and getting in shape are just a few of the benefits when preparing and practicing dance.

The 90/10 Principle

Discover the 90/10 Principle. It will change your life (at least the way you react to situations). What is this principle?

10% of life is made up of what happens to you. 90% of life is decided by how you react. What does this mean?

We really have no control over 10% of what happens to us. We cannot stop the car from breaking down. The plane will be late arriving, which throws our whole schedule off. A driver may cut us off in traffic. We have no control over this 10%. The other 90% is different. You determine the other 90%.

How? By your reaction. You cannot control a red light, but you can control your reaction. Don't let people fool you; YOU can control how you react.

Let's use an example. You are eating breakfast with your family. Your daughter knocks over a cup of coffee onto your business shirt. You have no control over what just what happened. What happens when the next will be determined by how you react.

You curse. You harshly scold your daughter for knocking the cup over.

She breaks down in tears. After scolding her, you turn to your spouse and criticize her for placing the cup too close to the edge of the table. A short verbal battle follows. You storm upstairs and change your shirt. Back downstairs, you find your daughter has been too busy crying to finish breakfast and get ready for school. She misses the bus. Your spouse must leave immediately for work.

You rush to the car and drive your daughter to school. Because you are late, you drive 40 miles an hour in a 30 mph speed limit. After a 15-minute delay and throwing $60 traffic fine away, you arrive at school. Your daughter runs into the building without saying goodbye. After arriving at the office 20 minutes late, you find you forgot your briefcase. Your day has started terrible. As it continues, it seems to get worse and worse. You look forward to coming home, When you arrive home, you find small wedge in your relationship with your spouse and daughter.

Why? Because of how you reacted in the morning. Why did you have a bad day?

A) Did the coffee cause it?

B) Did your daughter cause it?

C) Did the policeman cause it?

D) Did you cause it?

The answer is "D".

You had no control over what happened with the coffee. How you reacted in those 5 seconds is what caused your bad day. Here is what could have and should have happened.

Coffee splashes over you. Your daughter is about to cry. You gently say, "It's ok honey. You just need to be more careful next time". Grabbing a towel you rush upstairs. After grabbing a new shirt and your briefcase, you come back down in time to look through the window and see your child getting on the bus. She turns and waves. You arrive 5 minutes early and cheerfully greet the staff. Your boss comments on how good the day you are having.

Notice the difference? Two different scenarios. Both started the same. Both ended different.

Why? Because of how you REACTED. You really do not have any control over 10% of what happens. The other 90% was determined by your reaction.

Here are some ways to apply the 90/10 principle. If someone says something negative about you, don't be a sponge. Let the attack roll off like water on glass. You don't have to let the negative comment affect you! React properly and it will not ruin your day. A wrong reaction could result in losing a friend, being fired, getting stressed out etc.

How do you react if someone cuts you off in traffic? Do you lose your temper? Pound on the steering wheel? Do you curse? Does your blood pressure skyrocket? Do you try and bump them? WHO CARES if you arrive ten seconds later at work? Why let the cars ruin your drive? Remember the 90/10 principle, and do not worry about it.

You are told you lost your job. Why lose sleep and get irritated? It will work out. Use your worrying energy and time into finding another job. The plane is late; it is going to mangle your schedule for the day. Why take out your frustration on the flight attendant? She has no control over what is going on. Use your time to study, get to know the other passenger. Why get stressed out? It will just make things worse. Now you know the 90-10 principle. Apply it and you will be amazed at the results. You will lose nothing if you try it.

The 90-10 principle is incredible. Very few know and apply this principle.

The result? Millions of people are suffering from undeserved stress, trials, problems and heartache. We all must understand and apply the 90/10 principle.

It CAN change your life!!! [9]

Not making a squad can be discouraging. You can begin to pick yourself apart. You didn't make it because you weren't pretty enough or you didn't have the talent. Negative thinking has no room in this world. It is like any competition; it is the opinion of the judges. In one tryout, one person could not even make it through the first cut. In another audition, she could be selected to be on the team. It is all a matter of opinion and what an organization is looking for at that time.

"If things are not going well with you, begin your effort at correcting the situation by carefully examining the service you are rendering, and especially the spirit in which you are rendering it." Roger Babson

Many dynamics go into the look and image of a squad. The owner and director have a say in what that look is. Southern teams may favor blondes, while northern teams like brunettes. Some squads like thin girls, while others emphasize an "athletic" look. Do your research! Know what the director of the squad you are trying out for likes and dislikes!

"The important thing is this: to be able at any moment to sacrifice what you are for what you could become." Charles du Bos

---

[9] **Author : Stephen Covey (Management Guru)**

"Continuous effort--not strength or intelligence--is the key to unlocking our potential." Liane Cardes

"The difference between a successful person and others is not a lack of strength, not a lack of knowledge, but rather a lack of will." Vince Lombardi

The Path to a Dream

The path to a dream is paved with sacrifices and lined with determination.
And though it has many stumbling blocks along the way
And may go in more than one direction,
It is marked with faith.
It is traveled by belief and courage,
Persistence and hard work.
It is conquered with a willingness to face challenges and take chances,
To fail and try again and again.
Along the way, you may have to confront doubts, setbacks, and unfairness.
But when the path comes to an end,
You will find that there is no greater joy
Than making your dream come true.

Barbara Cage

"Character cannot be developed in ease and quiet. Only through experience of trial and suffering can the soul be strengthened, vision cleared, ambition inspired, and success achieved." Helen Keller

Why I Won't Give Up

You don't get to be a star without facing a lot of rejection first.

"An old friend once said to me, "Let's face it, Rainn- you and I, we're never going to be stars, so why don't we just quit?" I thought, "No. That can't be." And that made me redouble my efforts. I wanted to get better and better as an actor. You just can't give up. I mean, you just have to keep going." --Rainn Wilson

"There's some perverse pleasure in getting past failure. And also there's a freedom in knowing, "Ok, I don't have to be at the top of everybody's list." Every movie doesn't have to work. I'm fundamentally who I am. What's really going to determine my happiness is my friends, my family, and the people I love- and how I feel about myself." --Ben Affleck

"I was told to avoid the business all together because of rejection. People would say to me, "Don't you want to have a normal job and a normal family?" I guess that would be good advice for some people, but I wanted to act." --Jennifer Aniston

"I take rejection as someone blowing a bugle in my ear to wake me up and get me going, rather than retreat." --Sylvester Stallone

"You've got to love this business. You have to be able to take rejection." --Jessica Biel

"A rejection is nothing more than a necessary step in the pursuit of success." -- Bo Bennett, Businessman and Author

"You may not realize it when it happens, but a kick in the teeth may be the best thing in the world for you." -- Walt Disney, Entrepreneur and Dreamer

"Don't let anyone, or any rejection, keep you from what you want." -- Ashley Tisdale, Actress and Singer

"Through my illness I learned rejection. I was written off. That was the moment I thought, Okay, game on. No prisoners. Everybody's going down." -- Lance Armstrong, World Champion Cyclist and Cancer Survivor

"I would never have amounted to anything were it not for adversity. I was forced to come up the hard way." -- J. C. Penney, Department Store Founder

Chapter 8

Behind the Scenes

"What is the test of human character? It is probably this: that man will know how to be patient in the midst of hard circumstance, and can continue to be personally effective while living through whatever discouragements beset him and his companions."

Samuel Lymon Atwood

Here it is! The good, the bad, and the ugly!! Many know the surface of a dance team and rarely see the behind the scenes view. For example, many teams monitor weight and body fat composition. Weekly weigh-ins are the norm for most teams. Body image is a huge role for dance teams. Dancers are in small uniforms and "looking" the role is HUGE. Not looking good in the uniform is <u>not</u> an option. Many dance teams are sponsored by fitness facilities, which is a huge benefit. This is also where time management is important. By monitoring weight, dancers are subject to be benched or eventually dismissed from the team if expectations are not met.

Since weight is never any easy subject with women, it is easy to get offended when told to lose some weight or tone-up. Realize that this will *always* be a sensitive subject and toughen up! I have seen some of the smallest dancers told they need to tone up. Just because a person is skinny, does not mean they are not fat. They are called "Skinny Fat People". What this means is that they are naturally thin, but they are not healthy. Their eating habits are poor and/or they do not challenge their body physically on a daily basis. It is all about creating a healthy body for the years to come. Exercise and diet both play into a dancer's body. Motivating yourself with pictures and visualizing how you would look in the uniform can be a big push to get on that treadmill. The healthier you are, the better you will also feel.

Not only are you critiqued physically, but your dancing will also be evaluated. Being the best dancer on your high school squad or studio means nothing when you are at this level. Most of the girls that made the team were the best on THEIR team. The precision and perfection expected at the professional level is much greater. You are paid to be perfect.

As one of my coaches said, the way the public views you is completely different than reality. You don't have pimples, periods, or bad hair days. Once you enter that arena/stadium, it is about the game- not you. You will arrive 3-4 hours before the game, and you will be required to smile, no matter how bad of a day you have just had.

Chapter 9

The Big Picture

"Setting a goal is not the main thing. It is deciding how you will go about it and staying with that plan."

Tom Landry

While making it to the professional level is a huge goal, many dancers/cheerleaders have aspirations of creating more of themselves and setting even more goals for themselves. I have personally cheered with ladies that went on to open dance studios, become lawyers, go into the medical field, etc. etc. Here are a few examples of ladies that added to their resumes:

NFL cheerleaders who when on to bigger, better things:

Teri Hatcher [actress]: 49ers

Lisa Guerrero [sports reporter]: Rams

Jenilee Harrison [actress, Three's Company]: Rams

Tiffany Fallon [2005 Playmate of the Year]: Falcons

Stacy Keibler [WWE]: Ravens

Charisma Carpenter [actress, *Buffy*]: Chargers

Sarah Shahi [actress, *L Word*]: Cowboys

Jill Marie Jones [actress, *Girlfriends*]: Cowboys

Kristin Holt [TV personality, G4's *Cheat!* and *Poker Night*]: Cowboys

Kiana Tom [fitness shows]: Raiders

Tatiana Anderson [Fitness host]: Broncos

Anjelah Johnson [comedienne]: Raiders

Kristianna Nichols [1992 Mrs. America]: Redskins

Dallas Cowboys Cheerleaders Alumni:

Lezlie Deane - Actress in films such as Freddy's Dead: The Final Nightmare

Kristi Ferrell (DCC: 1978-1979) - Actress on the soap opera Guiding Light.

Tina Gayle (DCC: early 1980s) - Actress on the TV series CHiPs.

Tamara Glynn (DCC: 1991) - Actress in the horror film Halloween 5: The Revenge of Michael Myers.

Janet Gunn (DCC: early 1980s) - Actress on the TV series Silk Stalkings and Dark Justice.

Kristin Holt - Hostess of the video game show Cheat!, contestant on the first season of American Idol, and correspondent the next season. She also appeared on the cover of Stuff.

Jill Marie Jones - Starred in the TV series Girlfriends on The CW.

Bonnie-Jill Laflin - Host of ESPN2's Speed World, correspondent for ESPN's Cold Pizza morning show, cast member of Spike TV's Hotlines, and is one of the dance competition judges for NFL Network's NFL Cheerleader Playoffs.

Michelle Parma (DCC: 1995-1996) - Actress

Sarah Shahi (DCC: 1999-2000) - Cast member on the TV series The L Word. She appeared in the movie Old School. She was the Dallas Cowboys Cheerleaders 2000 Swimsuit Calendar Covergirl.

Sheila Slaughter Richey (DCC: late 80's) - Noted TV producer and Host for E! Entertainment Television, Lifetime Television & TNN.[10]

Houston Texan Cheerleaders

Using her great eye for talent, Alto, the Houston Texan Cheerleader Director, was keen enough to spot the talents of Stacy Keibler and hire her to be a Nitro Girl in 1999. Keibler performed as Skye and was later able to parlay the opportunity that she was given into the role of "Miss Hancock" and recently onto continued exposure on ABC's Dancing with the Stars. But it doesn't end there. Obviously blessed with ability to recognize talent, potential, beauty and ability, Alto is also responsible for bringing Diane and Elaine (aka the Coors Light Twins) to the attention of the world.[11]

---

[10] www.Dallascowboyscheerleaders.com

[11] http://www.houstontexans.com/team/FrontOfficebio.asp?front_office_id=112

NBA Dancers that went on to do big things:

Heat Dancer Alumni

Trista Rehn- ABC's original *Bachelorette*

Jessica Sutta - Pussycat Dolls sultry vocalist

Brooke Long- WWE's winner of the 2006 $250,000 Diva Search, Layla El, Suitcase #15 model, , of NBC's *Deal or No Deal*

Johanna Gomez- former host of the MUN2 show, *Fuzion*, current host of CABLETAP TV, Miami-Dade's Public Access TV Channel, and a reporter for "The Heat"[12]

Laker Girl Alumni

The most famous Laker Girl was Paula Abdul. After high school, while she was attending college at Cal State Northridge, Paula looked for a part time job. "A friend of mine heard about some auditions for the Laker Girls." She remembers. "I thought, sure, let's go try it out but, little did I know there would be hundreds of girls there trying out. I thought it would be a long shot to get selected, but

---

[12] http://www.nba.com/heat/dance/dancer_alumni.html

I tried out anyway." Little did Paula know, and expect, that the Lakers would call her back to tell her she was selected as one of the 12 girls on the squad. After Paula received the call to join the Laker Girls, she dropped out of college to pursue her career as an all around entertainer. This was an opportunity for her to do something she has always loved. Her mother, however, was not pleased with Paula's decision to quit college. "She was afraid that this (The Laker Girls) might not work out for me." She says. "I was very upset, but little did I know that her career would turn out this way. It turned out to be a good thing." Says Lorraine. The job for the Laker Girls did not pay much. Paula and the Laker Girls only made $50 a game, but she knew that a lot of celebrities in Hollywood attended Lakers games. She felt it would be good exposure and give her a chance to get noticed.[13]

---

[13] www.lakertickets.com/lakers-girls.htm

Chapter 10

Definite Do's & Positive Do Not's

Genuine good taste consists in saying much in few words, in choosing among our thoughts, in having order and arrangement in what we say, and in speaking with composure.

Francois de Salignac de la Mothe-Fenelon (1651-1715)

The Don'ts

Let's begin with the most common asked question: "Can the dancers/cheerleaders date the players?" For almost all teams, the answer is no. There are one or two professional teams that are the exception to this rule, but they are few and far between. You may, however, date players that are not on the same team you represent.

Having stated that this is a rule, I have to honestly say that every team that I have been on, at least one or two of the girls have fraternized with the players. The attraction is obvious: both parties have a lot in common. For example, the love of the sport and the high level of commitment to the team. The commitment to keep your body healthy and in constant shape. The drive to achieve high goals and be competitive enough to make it to that level in the first place. The sacrifice of having a hectic schedule.

The main question you have to ask yourself is this: Is it worth the risk of being caught? More than likely, it is not. Out of all of the girls that I know that took the risk, not one relationship ended in marriage. Players have been given the opportunity of a lifetime (just like you), and they are going to take full advantage of it. An athlete's career is very short as a professional. They are considered lucky if they are in the NBA or NFL for longer than 5 or 6 years. Their pocketbooks seem endless and their resources are plentiful. They are in their prime. Everyone wants a piece of them.

Here is what happens when a dancer is caught having "relations" with a player- so be warned! Usually, they are humiliated by the head office staff gaining knowledge of the affair. The director is then notified of the situation and more than likely forced to fire/kick the woman off of the squad. Her reputation is ruined and squads in the future will constantly hear about her actions while dragging her name through the mud. It will be hard for her to make another squad again (it is a very small dance world).

Now, you are probably asking yourself, "What repercussions do the players get?" I am glad you asked! Nothing. That's right. Maybe a small fine or a quick scolding, but that is about it. He doesn't lose his job or his reputation.

General Rule: There is no personal communication or dating of any players, coaches, or full-time staff personnel. Any activity or behavior, including phone calls, emails, excessive or improper fraternization in public or private places, which is or gives the appearance of a personal relationship or dating, will be cause for dismissal.

Never ask if you should do the routine "full out". You should always do it to the best of your ability unless the director advises otherwise.

Don't wear a crazy audition outfit. Stay within the guidelines of the audition attire requested. Different isn't always better!

Be careful not to compare yourself to others. It is a viscous cycle. You are your biggest competition. *"No one can make you feel inferior without your consent."* Eleanor Roosevelt.

Do not post questionable things or pictures on the internet. "Digital Dirt" can ruin your chances of future jobs.

Don't wait until the last minute to get your audition outfit. This will cause unneeded stress.

Do

- Do maintain a respectful reputation. *"Everything you say and do is the reflection of the inner you".* Think and speak intelligently.
- Be confident in your actions.
- Listen to the opinions of others.
- Make wise decisions under pressure.
- Be flexible and patient.
- Enjoy the opportunity.
- If you do travel overseas, know the international do's and don'ts. Use an interpreter if you do not know the language. Stay away from English slang, as it may not translate they way that you mean it! Learn at least the small words, such as hello and goodbye, to show you are at least trying. Keep things as simple as possible to avoid misunderstandings.

- Cover your tattoos.

- Practice applying makeup and blend it well to match your skin.

- Know the team you represent and the players. Who is the owner? Who did the team acquire in the latest draft pick? You may be quizzed by a fan on your feelings regarding the latest team news. To the fans, you are the organization and you need to represent your team well!

- Give everything you do 110%. *"Some succeed because they are destined to, but most succeed because they are determined to."*

Chapter 11

Teams

"Never doubt that a small group of thoughtful, committed people can change the world. Indeed, it's the only thing that ever has." Margaret Mead

NBA Dance Teams

(Summer Auditions)

Eastern Conference

Atlantic

Boston Celtics- "Celtics Dancers"

    Director: Marina Ortega
    www.nba.com/celtics/dancers

New Jersey Nets- "Nets Dancers"

    Director: Natasha Baron
    www.nba.com/nets/dancer
    For audition information, email entertainment@njnets.com

New York Knicks- "Knicks City Dancer"

    Coach/Entertainment Administrator: Danielle Mimnaugh
    Contact Info: danielle.mimnaugh@thegarden.com
    www.nyknickscitydancers.com

Philadelphia 76ers- "Sixers Dancers"

    Director: Debbie Apalucci
    www.nba.com/sixers/dance

Toronto Raptors- "Dance Pak"

>Director/Choreographer: Courtney Niven
>www.nba.com/raptors/0910_dancepak.html

Central

Chicago Bulls- "The Luvabulls"

>Director: Cathy Core
>www.nba.com/bulls/dance/luvabulls.html
>Notes: Must be 21 years old to audition

Cleveland Cavaliers- "Cavalier Girls"

>Choreographer: Vandana Patel
>www.nba.com/cavaliers/dance/cavalier_girls.html

Detriot Pistons- "Automotion"

>Director: Rebecca Girard   rgirard@palacenet.com
>www.nba.com/pistons/dance/automotion.html

Indiana Pacer- "Pacemates"
>Dance Teams Coordinator/Choreographer:
>Michelle Duggan
>http://www.nba.com/pacers/dance/home.html

Milwauke Bucks- "Energee!"

>Director: Lois Wagner Koepke
>Choreographer: Lynn Mothen
>http://www.nba.com/bucks/energee/energee_0910.html

Southeast

Atlanta Hawks- "A-Town Dancers"

> Dance Team & Talent Coordinator: Donni Frazier
> www.atowndancers.com/

Charlotte Bobcats- "Lady Cats"

> Coordinator, Special Appearances - Dave Stogdill
> www.nba.com/bobcats/lady_cats_0910.html

Miami Heat- "Heat Dancers"

> Entertainment Coordinator: Clara Stroude
> www.nba.com/heat/dance/index.html

Orlando Magic- "Magic Dancers"

> Manager: Jeanine Thomas
> Assistant Manager: Cherie LaRosa
> www.nba.com/magic/dancers/

Washington Wizards- "Wizard Girls"

> Director: Jessica Pikulski
> Assistant Directors: Brianne Ritzert & Kelly Owens
> www.nba.com/wizards/girls/

Western Conference

Southwest

Dallas Mavericks- "Mavs Dancers"

> Director: Mallory Mills
> www.nba.com/mavericks/dance/20092010_Dancers.html

Houston Rockets- "Rockets Power Dancers"

> Coach: Susie Boudwin
> www.nba.com.rockets/dance/0809_RPD_Website-283858-1664.html

Memphis Grizzlies- "Grizz Girls"

> Choreographer: Tamara Moore
> www.nba.com/grizzlies/dance

New Orleans Hornets- "Honeybees"

> Honeybee Manager/Choreographer: Ashley Deaton
> Contact: honeybees@hornets.com
> www.nba.com/hornets/dance

San Antonio Spurs- "Silver Dancers"

> Director: Raquel Torres
> www.nba.com/spurs/dance

Northwest

Denver Nuggets- "Nuggets Dancers"

>Director Amy Jo Wagner
>Contact Info: ajwagner@pepsicenter.com
>www.denvernuggetsdancers.com
>Notes: May be 16 years old to audition with a parent/legal guardian signature

Minnesota Timberwolves- "Timberwolves Dancers"

>Director: Erica Lentsch
>www.nba.com/timberwolves/dancers/

Portland Trail Blazers- "BlazerDancers"

>Performance Teams Manager: Michelle Woodard
>www.iamatrailblazersfan.com/Home/BlazerDancers/tabid/65/Default.aspx

Oklahoma City Thunder- "Thunder Girls"

>Dance Team Manager: Sabrina Ellison
>www.nba.com/thunder/thundergirls/index_0910.html

Utah Jazz- "Nu Skin Jazz Dancers"

>Director: Kelly Crane
>Contact Info: (801) 325-2587
>www.nba.com/jazz/dance/0910_dancers.html

Pacific

Golden State Warriors- "Warrior Girls"

> Director: Susan Hovey
> www.nba.com/warriors/dance/Warrior_Girl_Index.html

Los Angeles Clippers- "Spirit Dance Team"

> Director: Audrea Harris   Assistant: Cheryl Aure-Azurin
> www.nba.com/clippers/dance/spirit.html

Los Angeles Lakers

> Director of Game Operations& Entertainment: Lisa Estrada
> Contact Info: 310-426-6005
> www.nba.com/lakers/lakergirls/index.html

Phoenix Suns- "Suns Dancers"

> Dance Team Manager: Kari Herrick
> www.nba.com/suns/dance/0910_dancers_main.html

Sacramento Kings- "Sacramento Kings Dance Team"

> Dance Team Manager: Jenn Santich
> www.nba.com/kings/dance/Sacramento_Kings_Dancers.html

NFL Cheerleading Teams

(Spring Auditions)

AFC-North

Baltimore Ravens

> Cheerleader Coordinator: Tina Galdieri
> www.baltimoreravens.com/People/Cheer.aspx
> Tryouts: March

Cincinatti Bengals

> Director and Coordinator: Charlotte Jacobs
> www.bengals.com/cheerleaders/ben-gals.html
> Tryout: April & May

Cleveland Browns

> **No Cheerleaders**

Pittsburg Steelers

> **No Cheerleaders**

AFC-South

Houston Texans

> Cheerleaders Manager: Alto Gary
> http://www.houstontexans.com/Cheerleader09.asp
> Tryouts: April

Indianapolis Colts

>Cheerleader Coordinator: Theresa Pottratz
>www.colts.com/sub.cfm?page=cheer_home
>Tryouts: April & May
>Contact Info: (317) 808-5238 or
>theresa.pottratz@colts.nfl.net

Jacksonville Jaguars

>Manager: Christy Stechman Zynda
>www.jaguars.com/cheerleaders
>Tryouts: March

Tennessee Titans

>Director: Stacie Kinder
>www.titansonline.com/cheerleaders/index.html
>Tryouts: April

AFC-East

Buffalo Bills- "The Jills"

>Director: Stephanie Mateczun
>http://www.buffalojills.net
>Contact Info: Email: stephanie.mateczun@citcomm.com
>   Fax: 716.888.9773
>   Phone: 716.888.9798

Miami Dolphins

>Coordinator: Emily Snow
>www.miamidolphinscheerleaders.net/
>Tryouts: April

New England Patriots

>Cheerleader Director: Tracy Sormanti
>www.patriots.com/cheerleaders/
>Tryouts: February/ March

New York Jets - "Flight Crew"

>Director: Denise Garvey
>www.newyorkjets.com/flight_crew
>Tryouts: May

AFC-West

Denver Broncos

>Director: Teresa Shear
>www.denverbroncos.com/page.php?id=1667
>Tryouts: April/ May

Kansas City Chiefs

>Director: Stephanie Judah
>www.kcchiefs.com/cheerleaders/index.html
>Tryouts: January

Oakland Raiders- "Raiderettes"

> Raiderette Director/ Choreographer: Karen Kovac
> www.raiders.com/raiderettes/index.html
> Tryouts: April

San Diego Chargers- "Charger Girls"

> Team Director: Lisa Simmons
> www.chargers.com/charger-girls/index.html
> Tryouts: April

NFC-North

Chicago Bears

> **No Cheerleaders**

Detroit Lions

> **No Cheerleaders**

Green Bay Packers

> **No Cheerleaders**

Minnesota Vikings

> Head Coach and Coordinator: Tami Krause
> www.vikings.com/cheerleaders/index.html
> Tryouts: April

NFC-South

Atlanta Falcons

> Cheerleader Coordinator: Chato Waters
> www.atlantafalcons.com/People/Cheer_Roster.aspx
> Tryouts: April

Carolina Panthers- "Top Cats"

> Manager: Tina Becker   Choreographer: Richelle Grant
> www.panthers.com/topcats/index.html
> Tryouts: April & May

New Orleans Saints- "Saintsations"

> Director and Coordinator: Lesslee Fitzmorris
> http://www.neworleanssaints.com/saintsations/index.html
> Tryouts: April

Tampa Bay Buccaneers

> Coach: Sandy Charboneau
> www.buccaneers.com/cheerleaders/cheerauditions.aspx
> Tryouts: March & April

NFC-East

Dallas Cowboys

> Director: Kelli McGonagill Finglass
> Choreographer: Judy Trammell
> www.dallascowboyscheerleaders.com
> Tryouts: May

New York Giants

> **No Cheerleaders**

Philadelphia Eagles

> Director: Barbara Zahn   Choreographer: Suzy Zucker
> www.philadelphiaeagles.com/cheerleaders/index.asp
> Tryouts: April

Washington Redskins

> Director: Stephanie Jojokian
> www.redskins.com/gen/cheerleaders.jsp
> Tryouts: March

NFC-West

Arizona Cardinals

>Director: Heather Karberg
>www.azcardinals.com/cheerleaders/index.html
>Tryouts: April

San Francisco 49ers- "Gold Rush"

>Associate Director: Jamie Edmondson
>www.49ers.com/gold-rush/index.html
>Tryouts: March

Seattle Seahawks- "Sea Gals"

>Director: Sherri Thompson
>www.seahawks.com/sea-gals/index.html
>Tryouts: April

St. Louis Rams

>Entertainment Assistant & Cheerleader Coordinator:
>Theresa Mancini
>www.stlouisrams.com/Cheerleaders/
>Tryouts: April

Special Thanks

To my dear friends: Denise (aka Pocket Pal), Lara Lynn, Laura, Nicole, & Tina. I love you guys and truly cherish the moments we danced together and played together! I am looking forward to the future when we create a dance team at our nursing home!

Angel, Candice, Cristi, Jackie, Jessica, & Jodi: Thank you for being strong, independent women and for keeping me level-headed in high stress situations!

To my previous directors: For pushing me farther than I thought I could go (especially you Roz!)

Melissa & Molly: You were there in the beginning. I miss those late night choreography sessions in our apartment!

Lauren: Thanks for helping me think I could write this book! Your knowledge is priceless.

My family & Shawn: Thank you for believing in me and constantly supporting me. I love you!

All the college & professional teams I never made: Thank you for not taking me. At the time, I was crushed. However, looking back, it made me work harder. I became a better dancer, performer, and person. I would have never appreciated how special the opportunity was unless I had to work hard for it.

To My Students: Never let anyone tell you that you can't do something. Always work hard for the things you want in life.